# The Marijuana Chef Cookbook

S.T. Oner

GREEN CANDY PRESS

Published by Green Candy Press
San Francisco, CA

Copyright © 2013 S. T. Oner.

ISBN 978-1-937866-19-8

This book contains information about illegal substances, specifically the plant Cannabis Sativa and its derivative products. Green Candy Press would like to emphasize that cannabis is a controlled substance in North America and throughout much of the world. As such, the use and cultivation of cannabis can carry heavy penalties that may threaten an individual's liberty and livelihood.

The aim of the Publisher is to educate and entertain. Whatever the Publisher's view on the validity of current legislation, we do not in any way condone the use of prohibited substances.

Printed in China by Everbest Printing Co. through Four Colour Print Group.

Massively distributed by P.G.W.

Dedicated to NORML and everyone who has fought against the war on drug users.

# Contents

## Chapter 4

## Chapter 6

## Chapter 5

# Chapter 1

# Using Marijuana

There are many reasons why people choose to cook with marijuana, ranging from concerns about the health risks of smoking to the convenience of being able to carry the drug discreetly. Some medical marijuana users prefer eating the plant to smoking it, since many are not recreational drug users or cigarette smokers, and are therefore not accustomed to inhaling. The resultant high from eating marijuana can be a very pleasant experience in and of itself, and many people treating themselves with marijuana prefer to cook with the plant. When it is eaten, marijuana's effects range from mild to intense. While there have not been any recorded overdoses as a result of smoking marijuana, the effects of marijuana can be very intense when eaten. If not consumed in moderation, marijuana can induce dizziness, vomiting, and extreme anxiety. Knowing the potential effects that the drug can have on your body will help you weigh the benefits and risks of adding marijuana to your diet.

## THC: The Main Ingredient

The most potent of all the chemicals contained in marijuana is Tetrahydrocannabinol, or delta 9 THC. THC comes in many forms, called *isomers*. The THC isomers are subgroups of cannabinoids (monoterpene compounds) of which at least 50 have been isolated. The interaction of these cannabinoids causes a high that varies from strain to strain and gives each plant its distinct scent. For example, some highs tend to be more euphoric, while others cause drowsiness and relaxation. When marijuana is eaten, depending on the ingestion method, the psychoactive effects are dramatically different due to the various pathways through which the chemicals are absorbed into the body. When marijuana is smoked or inhaled, the THC transfuses almost instantly through the thousands of capillaries on the surface of the lungs. Increasing the contact with the capillaries increases the amount of THC in the smoke that will, in turn, be assimilated into the bloodstream. As a rule, marijuana smoke should be held in the lungs for at least twenty seconds — and up to fifty seconds — in order to absorb the maximum amount of THC.

Once it is in the bloodstream, the THC travels to the brain where it binds to certain receptors — receptors that appear to be designated specifically for this task. The presence of these receptors is often used to bolster the theory that an ancient genetic link exists between humans and marijuana. Another school of thought maintains that THC mimics the natural chemical anandamide, which also binds to these receptors. Anandamide is found in areas of the brain that regulate memory, coordination of movement, and emotions. Most prescribed drugs attempt to duplicate the body's own chemical processes but are decidedly not natural, whereas THC seems to be an all-natural drug that helps the body continue to function normally.

The direct transmission of marijuana from the lungs to the brain when it is smoked helps account for the quick onset of the high. This high wears off once the THC molecules no longer bind to the receptors. Ultimately, the same process occurs when marijuana is eaten, but there are important differences: the effects are multiplied. When marijuana is eaten, it is metabolized into a THC metabolite in the liver. The term *metabolized* simply describes the body's process of changing and using a substance to best suit its needs — it is the process of digesting food and absorbing vitamins. When THC is metabolized, it changes into a compound called 11-hydroxy-THC. This new compound is at least 15 percent more potent than delta 9 THC. Therefore, when 11-hydroxy-THC hits the brain, a more powerful high is induced. The initial effects can take a long time to set in, depending on how much food is already in the stomach, as well as the strength of the marijuana being used in the recipe. The effects, though, can last for up to five hours, or even longer. Since the food containing the drug may not be broken down all at once, the 11-hydroxy-THC high may surge in phases. When marijuana is eaten, users often report feeling an initial rush, followed by coming down, and then peaking once again. The change in THC's composition may account for the fact that vivid hallucinations and other wild effects are experienced after eating marijuana, whereas these reactions are relatively rare after inhaling it. The possibility of experiencing an intense buzz is often a favorable argument cited by devoted marijuana eaters. This probably accounts for so many groups using the plant for religious purposes — the experience can be surreal.

## Marijuana Mastery: Knowing the Risks

Now that you know how the drug works in your body, you should learn about the short- and long-term effects of marijuana use. One point cannot be stressed enough:

Do not dose people without their knowledge!

Make sure that anyone who is about to consume food containing marijuana is well aware of exactly what is involved. There are obvious reasons for this; the psychoactive properties of marijuana can be overwhelming even for experienced users if they are unaware of the oncoming effects. Also, there are times when being high for six to eight hours may not be convenient or welcome. Another thing to watch out for is inadvertently using too strong a dosage. Make sure that people know if the dish is particularly strong, as they might want to have just a small amount. It is a good idea when cooking cannabis to have some marijuana-free food lying around. Even though you may have just eaten, the munchies do still occur, especially a few hours into the high. At that point you probably will not be looking to become any higher, so eating some regular food would be wise. Plus, eating straight food — and sometimes taking a nap — can help relieve any unwanted reactions to the intensity of the high.

3

Cannabis highs are slightly unusual, as different strains can mimic the effects of many other psychoactive drugs. Some weed can seem speedy, while other weed is much more mellow. In addition, each person's reaction can vary according to his or her individual chemical makeup. Although there are distinctions between the sativa (energetic, light) and indica (soporific, tranquil) states, marijuana does not generally fit into any of the normal psychoactive groups of depressants, stimulants and hallucinogens. Instead, users fluctuate between these states, feeling at times energized and at other times sleepy. What will happen at any given time depends on many factors such as: what else has been consumed, how much marijuana was eaten, one's emotional state before using and so on. Also, the amount of previous exposure to the drug will change how the body functions under the influence. Long-term users tend not to suffer certain side effects that commonly afflict first-time or novice users, such as red eyes. Of course, the chance of experiencing side effects depends on the quality of the pot being consumed. Even though studies have been conducted to determine and identify what takes place within the body, the results are either contradictory or meaningless. Basically, a combination of positive and negative effects will occur. Feelings of euphoria are common, as are increased mental energy and awareness. People seem to be more in touch with their surroundings and may experience a distortion of the senses; people feel as though time is playing tricks on them. They also tend to feel a general sense of mirth — often resulting in fits of laughter.

These effects are not necessarily always positive. The increased awareness of one's social environment can cause paranoia, and distortion of time may lead to a sense of being out of control. However, it should be noted that a good deal of the paranoia is probably due to the fact that one is committing an illegal act. It can be upsetting to zone out and forget where things are, or forget what you were saying. Inexperienced smokers will often notice an increase in their heart rate. This can be accompanied by anxiety and in some cases panic. Every drug, including alcohol and caffeine, has side effects. It is important to know what effects may occur and to decide whether or not you believe that the drug is worth taking. The answer to this question will differ for everyone, but it is something that should be considered before ingesting any type of drug.

## The Truth Is Out There: Marijuana Research

Due to marijuana's status as a "Schedule I" narcotic, it has been next to impossible to study the drug in a scientific manner for much of the last century. This has lead to contradictory, misleading and often anecdotal information being spread as the gospel truth. In fact, attempts to research marijuana's long-term effects have produced mostly inconclusive data from sources that have staked out clear positions. However, it can be safely said that repeated long-term use of the drug will have lasting effects on a person's brain and respiratory system. No one fully understands how the brain reacts to cannabis; however, brain scans show that the brain of a user is different after a few years of marijuana use when compared to that of a nonuser. Exactly what this information implies is unknown. There is no proof that marijuana causes the death of brain cells, and it is unlikely that it does so to the same degree as alcohol because it would therefore be measurable, as is the case when alcohol is consumed. Even if brain cell loss could be proven, there is no further link establishing a fundamental change in a person's behavior or intelligence. The same can be said about the rumored links between marijuana and mental illness. Though some people definitely "wig out" while on the drug, this behavior subsides as soon as the marijuana has ceased binding to the receptors — when the person has "come down."

Although marijuana has been never been shown to be physically addictive, there is probably a level of social addiction that occurs. In these cases, users will seek out cannabis because they have habitually done so — not to simply satisfy a physical craving. Some studies have tried to demonstrate that users become more aggressive and irritable when deprived of the drug. This could very well be true; coffee drinkers tend to experience similar reactions when lacking caffeine. However, the rush to ban caffeine has not even begun. Some studies claim that long-term users suffer from what has been labeled "amotivational syndrome." This probably has as much to do with the particular user as it does with THC levels.

It is often reported that consuming the plant can lead to either a reduced libido and/or impotency. There is no basis to this claim of impotency whatsoever. But, like coffee drinkers, male cannabis users have been shown to produce a relatively higher amount of two-tailed sperm. When viewed as a percentage of the total amount of sperm produced, however, they are statistically insignificant. The typical human male produces millions of sperm in one day, and barring any preexisting conditions, will produce millions more the next day.

## Common Effects of Marijuana

- Red eyes
- Increase in appetite
- Altered sense of time
- Dry mouth
- Heightening of senses
- Laughter, general mirth
- Anxiety
- Drowsiness

- Muscle relaxation
- Vertigo, dizziness
- Vomiting
- A depressed feeling
- Relaxed inhibitions
- Paranoia
- Hallucinations
- Confusion

An important thing to consider when hearing claims and reading studies about marijuana is that most research has been performed on heavy users. Since the definition of the "recreational user" varies for everyone, and since we each have a unique biochemistry, it would be foolhardy to accept any study (whether favorable or negative) as the final word. Much more research is needed, and in some countries — especially Europe — that work is now underway.

## To Eat or Not to Eat?

Concerns about the safety of smoking are very high, which is one reason why people prefer to cook with marijuana. The smoke from a joint contains three times more tar than a standard cigarette, and five times more carbon monoxide. This information, combined with the fact that marijuana smoke hits the lungs at a higher temperature, leads people to believe that cannabis smoke is more likely to cause respiratory disease or cancer of the lungs than tobacco smoke. However, marijuana does not contain nicotine — a drug that is thought to be even more addictive than heroin. While marijuana smoking is definitely not "healthy," it should be noted that most pot smokers do not have the same "pack-a-day" habits as cigarette smokers. One way to counteract the toxins contained in the smoke is to use a bong or water pipe, which can help filter out some of the impurities and carcinogens. However, bongs are not very easy to conceal, and in many places the legal ramifications of having paraphernalia are as severe as having the plant in one's possession.

Of course nothing will minimize the effect of smoking as much as simply not smoking at all. Smoking pot may not be as convenient as eating it, especially for medicinal users, since the effects wear off sooner. It is not always possible to maintain your high if you smoke pot, especially if you are in a public place. There are many events that might be enhanced by a marijuana high, such as concerts, movies, and trips to the zoo, but these are not good places to light up. However, if you eat cannabis, there will be nothing to confiscate, and your high will continue.

## Marijuana as Medicine

People who use the marijuana plant for medical purposes (especially to relieve constant pain) often have to smoke up to five or six joints a day — a habit that may not be easily concealed from coworkers, the authorities, and others who might disapprove. Obviously if you are on the job, you don't want the entire staff to know about your marijuana use even if the drug has been prescribed by a doctor to alleviate your suffering. Many people still have not accepted the use of marijuana as medicine, and combating other people's personal bias when you are in pain is an unwelcome, additional stress. People who suffer from chronic pain may want to eat marijuana because the long-lasting high enables muscle relaxation and relief. Recreational users typically want a high to kick in quickly. However, medical users might actually want a slower release of the drug into their system, since it enables the high to last longer. This may mitigate the extreme of the high, but consistent relief is what some consider most important. To achieve this, consider eating doses of marijuana with larger serving sizes. As the body breaks down the food, the marijuana will be released in stages — a process very similar to a "time-release" capsule.

People have found marijuana to be effective in the treatment and relief of numerous ailments and terminal conditions. One of the first illnesses that pot was legally made available for was glaucoma. Marijuana has been proven effective in reducing ocular pressure, a condition that damages the eye over time. Glaucoma is the second leading cause of blindness in the United States, and most sufferers of the disease are not physically helped by the medications currently available. Unfortunately, most of these people do not live in areas where their doctors can prescribe marijuana. There are many glaucoma patients who credit their remaining eyesight to marijuana use. Other advocates include cancer patients undergoing chemotherapy, who use cannabis to stimulate their appetites. Their increased appetite helps them maintain the weight and strength to fight their illness. People living with multiple sclerosis, AIDS, and chronic migraines are all helped by marijuana's properties. Since most medicinal users don't want to smoke, for obvious health reasons, eating marijuana is their best option.

People may also choose to eat marijuana simply for economic reasons. Although you certainly can cook the flowers and the bud of the plant, it is just as effective to cook with the plant's leaves. The leaves are useless to the grower once the plant is harvested, and they have to be pruned off the plant. Be aware that leaves are still just as dangerous to have in your possession — the penalties for a pound of leaf are the same as those for a pound of bud — so the grower has an incentive to get rid of the leaves as soon as possible. But, because the leaves are harsh to smoke and are not nearly as high in THC, they are not very valuable and are often given away or destroyed as soon as possible. When cooked, the leaves will be stronger than their equivalent weight in buds.

## Chapter 2

# Marijuana Cooking Basics

Marijuana, unlike most other drugs, is oil-based. It is essential to know this distinction when cooking with the drug; it is important to ensure that the psychoactive properties are evenly distributed through the food. The THC of a marijuana plant is contained in the capitate glands that cover its leaves, but the flowers contain the highest density of the drug. Using an oil product, such as butter or vegetable oil, does a fine job of dissolving the capitate glands and releasing the THC. So, it follows that making pot tea solely with water will not be as effective unless milk or honey is also used. There are two basic ways to break down the plant for cooking: one is to make flour out of the leaves, and the other is to make marijuana leaf butter. To make the flour, you should grind very dry leaves in a food processor or coffee grinder until they are very fine. To make marijuana butter, simply combine about a pound of butter for every four ounces of marijuana leaf. Be sure to melt it down completely, and then strain the liquid from the mixture and store it in the refrigerator. It is common for people to add marijuana to desserts because desserts have a high fat content, usually have small serving sizes, and are very tasty in their own right. The fat is the key: it dissolves the plant's capitate glands and helps maintain even distribution throughout the food. When the serving size is smaller, the high will take effect much faster since there is less food to digest.

Of course, the main thing to worry about when cooking with marijuana is that the dosage is correct — ingesting too much of the drug can leave you incapacitated. Since your aim is for people to have a good time, as a good cook you should pay special attention to dosage guidelines. Additionally, you want to make sure that the dose is spread out evenly in the food. Dosage has as much to do with the quality of the plant as it does with the individual body weights of the people who are eating the food, as well as their experiences with marijuana. Generally speaking, the concentration of THC in a plant is between 4 and 8 percent, though some high-grade products could be as high as 10 percent. Inexperienced users should stay within the lower ranges, eating less than 1/2 gram per serving. More experienced users can eat stronger servings, but should still be careful as they approach 1 1/2 grams. As a general rule, eating 1 gram of pot will bring you to a peak in about two hours. Your peak will likely last for a couple of hours and then you'll start to come down. All in all, the effects of the marijuana will be felt for a total of seven hours. Be especially careful with dosage when substituting pot butter in a straight recipe, or one that does not call for marijuana. In these cases, the tendency might be to add a little more than necessary, which you should avoid doing. Remember — you can always eat more.

# Marijuana Butter

Marijuana Butter can be used in any number of recipes, from desserts to entrees and appetizers. For best results, Marijuana Butter should be prepared one full day before using.

1 Grind the marijuana up well, using a coffee grinder if possible.

2 Combine the butter and marijuana in a large crock pot.

3 Add enough water to cover the bud and butter by a couple of inches.

4 Turn the crock pot on low and allow the butter to melt, then stir.

5 Simmer on the lowest heat for 3 hours or longer to attain maximum extraction.

6 Turn off the crock pot and allow mixture to cool slightly.

7 Pour the mixture through a fine mesh strainer lined with cheesecloth into a glass bowl.

8 Press the remaining liquid from the marijuana.

9 Refrigerate for a few hours or overnight, until the butter has solidified on top of the water.

10 Lift the butter away from the water and drain the water away, then remelt the butter gently in a crock pot or pan.

11 Divide into several smaller containers ready for use.

12 Freeze until needed.

**Recommended Dosage**

Approximately ½ ounce of bud for every 1 pound of butter

**Preparation Time**

5 minutes

**Cooking Time**

3 hours

# Marijuana Coconut Oil

Marijuana Coconut Oil is an easy vegan alternative to Marijuana Butter, made much the same way and used in a similar fashion. If you avoid dairy in your diet, or are looking for a healthier extraction method, give this a try. It's delicious too!

1 Grind the marijuana up well, using a coffee grinder if possible.

2 Pour a couple of inches of water into your crock pot, and set the heat to low.

3 Add the room-temperature coconut oil into the crock pot and allow it to melt into the water.

4 When melted, add the ground marijuana and stir.

5 Lower the heat and simmer for 3 hours or longer to attain maximum extraction.

6 Turn off the crock pot and allow mixture to cool slightly.

7 Pour the mixture through a fine mesh strainer lined with cheesecloth into a glass bowl.

8 Press the remaining liquid from the marijuana.

9 Refrigerate for a few hours or overnight, until the coconut oil has solidified on top of the water.

10 Lift the solidified oil away from the water and drain the water away, then remelt the oil gently in a crock pot or pan.

11 Divide into several smaller containers ready for use.

12 Freeze or keep in the fridge until needed.

**Recommended Dosage**

Approximately ½ ounce of bud for every 450 gram / 2 cups of coconut oil

**Preparation Time**

5 minutes

**Cooking Time**

3 hours

# Marijuana Flour

An easy way to prepare marijuana for baking is to process either leaf or bud into flour. The difference between leaf and bud is that the strength is different so the dosage will differ. Marijuana Flour can then be added to recipes.

**Recommended Dosage**
½ to 2 grams per serving

**Preparation Time**
10 minutes

1 Make sure that the bud and/or leaf is dry enough to crumble easily between your fingers.

2 Grind the marijuana in a food processor or coffee grinder to a powder-like consistency. A food processor might be best for larger quantities.

3 Place a sieve over a bowl and with the back of a wooden spoon, work the marijuana flour through the sieve to break down larger stubborn pieces.

4 You might notice a fine dust being thrown up during the process. This is precious, potent stuff, rich in THC, so hang on to it!

5 Store in an airtight container and refrigerate.

# Marijuana Alcohol

Marijuana Alcohol can be used to create an intoxicating and mouthwatering array of beverages. It should be prepared at least two weeks before using. Remember not to drink too much; one cocktail should be more than enough.

**Recommended Dosage**

2 ounces of leaf per liter of vodka

**Preparation Time**

5 minutes

**Cooking Times**

5 minutes to mix, at least 2 weeks to stand

1 Trim 2 ounces of leaves off their stems.

2 Add them to a mason jar with the vodka, making sure all the leaves are submerged.

3 Label the jar with the date, so you don't forget when you started it.

4 Place the jar into a cool, dark place and wait for a minimum of 2 weeks.

5 When the time is up, strain the vodka through a sieve into a glass bowl.

6 Store into a small jar or tincture bottle with eyedropper. Use sparingly.

## Chapter 3

# Dessert First

If you're like me, dessert is the food you reach for first when you're enjoying marijuana in any form. It seemed perfectly natural, then, to blend marijuana and the following dessert classics to create the perfect treat to satisfy both your marijuana craving and the munchies. Take it from me, the Marijuana Chef: when you're cooking with cannabis, always enjoy your Dessert First!

# Gone Bananas Bread

You'll go ape for this tasty treat!

1 Preheat oven to 350°F/175°C.

2 Butter and flour a 9 x 5 x 2½-inch metal loaf pan.

3 In a medium bowl, stir the flour, baking soda, baking powder and salt together.

4 Combine the chocolate chips (and walnuts, if using) in a small bowl then add 1 tablespoon of flour mixture, and toss to coat.

5 Beat butter in a large bowl until fluffy. Gradually add the sugar, beating until well blended.

6 Beat in the eggs one at a time.

## Ingredients

⅓ cup of Marijuana Butter

1 ½ cups of all-purpose flour

1 teaspoon of baking powder

1 teaspoon of baking soda

¼ teaspoon of salt

¾ cup of semisweet chocolate chips

¾ cup of walnuts, toasted, chopped (optional)

⅓ cup of unsalted butter, room temperature

1 cup of sugar

2 large eggs

1 cup of mashed ripe bananas

1 ½ teaspoons of vanilla extract

2 tablespoons of fresh lemon juice

## Servings

Makes one 9-inch loaf that makes 10 slices

## Recommended Dosage

1 slice

## Preparation Time

10 minutes

## Cooking Time

Approximately 1 hour

**7** Beat in mashed bananas, lemon juice and vanilla extract.

**8** Beat in the flour mixture.

**9** Spoon ⅓ of the batter into the prepared pan and sprinkle with half of the nut mixture.

**10** Spoon ⅓ of the batter over the top, then sprinkle with the remaining nut mixture.

**11** Cover with the remaining batter, then run a knife through the batter in a zigzag pattern.

**12** Bake until a fork or knife inserted into the center of the loaf comes out clean. This should take 1 hour and 5 minutes.

**13** Turn it onto a rack and allow it to cool.

# Pumpkin Muffins

Get smashed out of your pumpkin with these muffins.

1 Preheat oven to 350°F/175°C.

2 Mix together the flour, baking soda, baking powder, salt, cinnamon, ginger, nutmeg and allspice in a medium bowl and set aside.

3 In a large bowl, whisk together the light brown sugar, granulated sugar, Marijuana Butter, normal butter and eggs.

## Ingredients

⅓ cup of Marijuana Butter

⅓ cup of butter

2 cups of all-purpose flour

1 teaspoon of baking soda

1 teaspoon of baking powder

1 teaspoon of salt

1 teaspoon of ground cinnamon

1 teaspoon of ground ginger

¼ teaspoon of ground nutmeg

¼ teaspoon of ground allspice

1 cup of packed light brown sugar

1 cup of granulated sugar

4 large eggs, lightly beaten

1 15-ounce can of pumpkin puree

## Servings

Makes 12 to 14 muffins

## Recommended Dosage

1 muffin

## Preparation Time

15 minutes

## Cooking Time

20 to 25 minutes

4 Add the dry mixture and mix until smooth.

5 Whisk in the pumpkin puree.

6 Place paper liners in your muffin tray and fill halfway with batter.

7 Bake until the tops of the muffins spring back when touched, and a toothpick inserted in the center comes out clean. This should take 20 to 25 minutes.

8 Leave to cool, then chow down!

# Peanut Budder Cups

You'll be butterly smashed!

1 Grease a cupcake tray or mini-cupcake tray, covering the whole inside of each cup.

2 Melt half the chocolate in a double boiler, being careful not to burn it, and stir in half the Marijuana Butter.

3 Divide the melted chocolate between the cupcake cups, just covering the bottom of each one.

4 Put the pan into the freezer.

5 In a bowl, cream together the peanut butter and powdered sugar.

6 Roll the peanut butter mixture into 12 or 24 little balls, so there's one per cup.

7 When the chocolate has frozen, remove from the freezer and press 1 ball into each cup, making sure it doesn't touch the sides.

8 Melt the rest of the chocolate, adding in the remaining Marijuana Butter, and stir until combined.

9 Divide between the cups evenly, making sure the chocolate covers the peanut butter, and swirl with your finger to create a nice effect on top.

10 Freeze for an hour, then store them in the fridge until ready to eat!

## Ingredients

¼ cup of Marijuana Butter

3 cups of chocolate chips

¼ cup of powdered sugar

1 cup of peanut butter

Oil

## Servings

12 large cups or 24 small ones

## Recommended Dosage

2 large cups or 4 small ones

## Preparation Time

15 minutes

## Cooking Time

1 hour 30 minutes, with the hour being freezing time

# Sweet Sensations Sugar Cookies

Surrender to the sugar high!

**1** Preheat oven to 350°F/175°C.

**2** In a mixer or with a fork or whisk, cream together the Marijuana Butter, unsalted butter and sugar until light and fluffy.

**3** Add in the egg, milk and vanilla extract and mix until combined.

**4** In a separate bowl, sift together the flour, salt and baking powder.

**5** Stir the flour mixture into the butter mixture until just combined.

**6** Transfer the dough onto a floured surface and work into a ball.

**7** Cover with Saran wrap and place in the refrigerator for 1 hour.

**8** Remove the dough from the refrigerator and allow it to soften slightly.

**9** Pinch off teaspoon-sized pieces of dough and roll into a ball, then place onto a cookie sheet lined with parchment paper and flatten slightly. Repeat for all the dough.

**10** Alternatively, roll out to ¼-inch thickness and use cookie cutters to cut into shapes, then place on the cookie sheet.

**11** Bake for 8 to 10 minutes, until lightly browned, then transfer to wire racks to cool.

**12** Decorate with icing or just serve as they are.

## Ingredients

- 6 tablespoons of Marijuana Butter
- 2 tablespoons of unsalted butter
- 2 cups of all-purpose flour
- ¼ teaspoon of salt
- ½ teaspoon of baking powder
- 1 cup of sugar
- 1 large egg
- 2 tablespoons of milk
- ½ teaspoon of vanilla extract

## Servings

24 cookies

## Recommended Dosage

1 cookie

## Preparation Time

15 minutes

## Cooking Time

1 hours to chill, 10 minutes for cooking

# Dirty Date Cookies

Get down and dirty with these date cookies.

1 Preheat oven to 350°F/175°C.

2 Chop the dates, then in a bowl, stir together the melted Marijuana Butter and brown sugar.

3 Add in the flour and baking soda.

4 Beat the egg in a cup, then add it to the flour mixture along with the vanilla extract, chopped dates and the oats.

5 Stir well, then drop tablespoons of the dough onto a large ungreased baking sheet (you might need to use 2). Leave a space of at least 2 inches between each cookie.

6 Bake for 18 to 20 minutes, until the cookies are golden brown.

7 Cool and enjoy!

**Ingredients**

½ cup of Marijuana Butter, melted

1 ¼ cups of pitted dates

³/₄ cup of packed light brown sugar

²/₃ cup of all-purpose flour

³/₄ teaspoon of baking soda

1 large egg

1 teaspoon of vanilla extract

1 ½ cups of quick-cooking oats

**Servings**

24 cookies

**Recommended Dosage**

1 cookie

**Preparation Time**

15 minutes

**Cooking Time**

18 to 20 minutes

# Outrageous Oatmeal Chip Cookies

So good they oat to be illegal!

1 Preheat oven to 350°F/175°C.

2 In a large bowl, beat together the brown sugar, Marijuana Butter, unsalted butter and sugar until creamy.

3 Add the eggs, milk and vanilla and beat well.

4 Stir in the flour, baking soda and salt.

5 Mix in the oatmeal and chocolate chips.

6 Drop by teaspoonfuls onto an ungreased baking sheet and bake for 10 to 12 minutes or until cookies start to brown.

7 Cool slightly before removing them from the baking sheet.

## Ingredients

½ cup of Marijuana Butter

1¼ cups of brown sugar, firmly packed

¼ cup of butter, softened

½ cup of sugar

2 eggs

2 tablespoons of 2 percent milk

2 teaspoons of vanilla

1¾ cups of flour

1 teaspoon of baking soda

1 teaspoon of salt

2½ cups of quick-cooking oatmeal

12 ounces of semisweet chocolate chips

## Servings

24 cookies

## Recommended Dosage

1 cookie

## Preparation Time

15 minutes

## Cooking Time

10 to 12 minutes

# Nutty Peanut Butter Cookies

Nothing could be better!

1 Preheat oven to 375°F/190°C.

2 In a large bowl, cream together the Marijuana Butter, plain butter and the sugars.

## Ingredients

½ cup of Marijuana Butter

¼ cup of butter

½ cup of brown sugar

½ cup of white sugar

1 cup of peanut butter

1 ½ cup of flour

1 egg

1 teaspoon of salt

½ teaspoon of baking soda

½ teaspoon of vanilla
extract

## Servings

30 cookies

## Recommended Dosage

1 cookie

## Preparation Time

15 minutes

## Cooking Time

10 to 15 minutes

3 Add the egg, peanut butter, salt and baking soda.

4 Mix the flour into the batter, and add the vanilla extract.

5 Roll the dough into 30 small balls and flatten with a fork dipped in water.

6 Bake for 10 to 15 minutes.

# Crazed Carrot Cake

420 vision!

1 Preheat oven to 325°F/160°C.

2 Stir the flour, sugar, baking soda, cinnamon and salt into a mixing bowl.

3 Mix in the grated carrots, vanilla extract and eggs.

4 Beat the mixture and slowly add oil.

5 Pour the batter into a greased 8 x 12-inch pan, or two 8-inch diameter pans.

6 Bake for 35 to 45 minutes, or until a tester placed in the center comes out clean.

## Ingredients

2 cups of flour

2 cups of sugar

2 teaspoons of baking soda

2 teaspoons of cinnamon

1 teaspoon of salt

3 cups of grated carrots

4 eggs

1 teaspoon of vanilla extract

1 ¼ cups of vegetable oil

Frosting:

8 ounces of cream cheese

2 tablespoons of butter

½ cup of Marijuana Butter

1 tablespoon of vanilla
   extract

3 ¾ cups of powdered
   sugar

## Servings

1 cake, serves 20

## Recommended Dosage

1 slice

## Preparation Time

30 minutes

## Cooking Time

35 to 35 minutes

## Frosting directions

1 Beat the cream cheese, butter, Marijuana Butter and vanilla extract together.

2 While beating, add the powdered sugars in thirds.

3 Frost the cake, or the top of the cake and between the layers if you made two layers, and enjoy!

# "Choc-ful-'o-Pot" Chocolate Chip Cookies

Melts in your mouth, not in your hands!

1 Preheat oven to 350°F/175°C.

2 Cream the butter, Marijuana Butter and sugars together until smooth.

3 Beat in the eggs one at a time, with a pinch of the flour.

4 Stir in the vanilla.

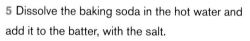

## Ingredients

½ cup of butter, softened

½ cup of Marijuana Butter

1 cup of packed brown
   sugar

1 cup of white sugar

2 eggs

2 teaspoons of vanilla
   extract

3 cups of all-purpose flour

½ teaspoon of salt

1 teaspoon of baking soda

2 teaspoons of hot water

2 cups of semisweet
   chocolate chips

1 cup of chopped walnuts
   (optional)

## Servings

24 cookies

## Recommended Dosage

1 cookie

## Preparation Time

20 minutes

## Cooking Time

10 minutes

5 Dissolve the baking soda in the hot water and add it to the batter, with the salt.

6 Stir in the flour, chocolate chips and nuts (if using).

7 Drop large spoonfuls of batter onto an ungreased baking tray.

8 Bake for about 10 minutes, or until the edges are slightly browned.

# Baked Brownies

Unlike Mom used to make.

1 Preheat oven to 350°F/175°C.

2 Grease a 13 x 9-inch pan.

3 Beat the eggs, butter, sugar and vanilla extract in a large bowl.

4 Mix in the cocoa, flour, Marijuana Flour, salt and baking powder and blend.

## Ingredients

³/₄ cup of melted butter

1 ½ teaspoons of vanilla extract

1 ½ cups of sugar

3 eggs

½ cup of Hershey's cocoa (or a comparable brand)

½ cup of flour

⅓ cup of Marijuana Flour

½ teaspoon of baking powder

1 cup of chopped nuts (optional)

1 cup of chocolate chips

## Servings

12 brownies

## Recommended Dosage

1 brownie

## Preparation Time

15 minutes

## Cooking Time

20 to 22 minutes

5 Stir in the nuts (if using) and the chocolate chips.

6 Pour into a pan and bake for 20 to 22 minutes.

7 Cool 'em, cut 'em and eat 'em up!

# Stoner Scones

Enjoy "high" tea every day!

1 Preheat oven to 400°F/200°C.

2 Mix together the flour, 1/3 cup of the sugar, baking powder and baking soda.

3 Cut the Marijuana Butter into the flour mixture, eventually using your fingers to rub the butter into the flour until it resembles breadcrumbs.

4 In a separate bowl, whisk the sour cream and egg together.

5 Stir the sour cream mixture into the flour mixture until it begins to form a

## Ingredients

½ cup of Marijuana Butter, cold

2 cups of all-purpose flour

⅓ cup of powdered sugar

1 teaspoon of baking powder

¼ teaspoon of baking soda

½ cup of raisins

½ cup of sour cream

1 large egg

## Servings

8

## Recommended Dosage

1 scone

## Preparation Time

15 minutes

## Cooking Time

20 minutes

dough. Press the dough together into a ball.

6 Stir the raisins into the dough and knead it to combine evenly.

7 Turn out onto a floured surface and divide the dough into 8 portions. Pat into discs just less than an inch thick.

8 Place onto a greased cookie sheet and bake for 15 minutes, until golden.

9 Serve with cream, jam and a cup of tea!

# Chapter 4

# Soups and Starters

There really is nothing more comforting on a cold winter's day than a soup laced with your favorite strain; maybe a Cream of Cannabis laced with Exodus Cheese, or Off Your Noodle Soup with a hint of OG Kush. Or, if you're serving up a stoner dinner party, with the starters in this sections you can be sure that once you've hit the main course, your guests are ravenous for more…and more, and more!

# Off Your Noodle Soup

## Just what the doctor ordered!

1 In a large pot, melt the butter and Marijuana Butter over a low heat.

2 Add the carrots, celery, onions and pepper.

3 Cook and stir over a medium heat for about 5 minutes.

4 Add the mushrooms and cook for 2 to 3 more minutes or until the carrots are tender.

5 Add the broth and bring to a simmer.

6 Add the chicken and noodles.

7 Simmer for 2 to 3 minutes longer.

8 Garnish with the fresh herbs and serve.

### Ingredients

⅓ cup of butter

2 tablespoons of Marijuana Butter

1 cup of carrots, diced

1 cup of celery, diced

½ cup of onion, chopped

½ teaspoon of freshly ground pepper

1¼ cups of white mushrooms, sliced

6 cups of chicken broth

1 cup of cooked chicken cubes

2 cups of wide egg noodles, cooked

2 to 3 tablespoons of fresh dill or parsley, chopped

### Servings

6

### Recommended Dosage

1½ cups

### Preparation Time

20 minutes

### Cooking Time

20 to 22 minutes

# Cream of Cannabis Soup

Good to the last drop!

1 Trim the roots and the leaves from leeks, leaving only the white and about 2 inches of the green sections.

2 Rinse well, split lengthwise and slice cross-wise (about ½-inch thick). Sauté the leeks in butter in a large pan over a low heat for about 10 minutes.

3 Stir in the chicken broth, potatoes, salt and pepper and bring to a boil over a high heat.

4 Trim off and discard the stem ends of the asparagus.

5 Chop the remaining asparagus into 1-inch pieces and add to the boiling soup.

6 Reduce the heat and simmer uncovered for about 10 minutes or until vegetables are tender.

7 Transfer soup to a food processor or blender and process until pureed.

8 Return the soup to a clean saucepan.

9 Stir in the cream and heat.

10 Serve with a little cream on top of the soup.

**Ingredients**

2 large leeks

2 tablespoons of butter

2 tablespoons of Marijuana Butter

4 cups of ready-to-serve chicken broth

2 medium potatoes, peeled and diced

½ teaspoon of salt

½ teaspoon of pepper

20 spears of asparagus

½ cup of whipping cream

**Servings**

6

**Recommended Dosage**

1 ¼ cups

**Preparation Time**

5 minutes

**Cooking Time**

45 to 50 minutes

# Tofu Asparagus Hash

Tip your hat to this mouthwatering meal.

1 Cut the bottom third off the asparagus spears, chop into thin pieces then place them into a steamer or in a sieve above a pan of simmering water and steam for 10 minutes until tender.
2 In a bowl, break the tofu up with a fork until it resembles scrambled eggs.

## Ingredients

600 grams of firm tofu

2 tablespoons of Marijuana
Butter

16 spears of asparagus

1 medium onion, diced

3 tablespoons of soy sauce

2 teaspoons of cumin

2 teaspoons of coriander

1 teaspoon of turmeric

3 cloves of garlic

## Servings
4

## Recommended Dosage
1 serving

## Preparation Time
5 minutes

## Cooking Time
20 minutes

3 Stir in the soy sauce, cumin, coriander and turmeric and set aside.

4 Melt the Marijuana Butter in a frying pan and sauté the garlic and onion for 3 minutes.

5 Add the tofu mixture to the pan and heat, stirring often, for 5 to 7 minutes.

6 Add in the asparagus and stir to combine.

7 Serve with crusty bread.

# Vinaigrette

You don't always make friends with salad,
but you will with this one.

**1** Start by slowly simmering the oil and shake in a pan over medium low
for 15 to 30 minutes.
**2** Remove from the heat, cool and strain.

### Ingredients
½ ounce of shake

¼ cup of balsamic vinegar

½ cup of olive oil

2 cloves of garlic

1 shallot, diced

1 tablespoon of Dijon
   mustard

1 tablespoon of maple
   syrup

Basil, oregano, parsley and
   rosemary to taste

Pinch of salt and pepper

### Servings
4

### Recommended Dosage
1 serving

### Preparation Time
10 minutes

### Cooking Time
15 to 30 minutes

3 Discard the shake and combine the oil,
vinegar and all the other ingredients together in
a bowl.

4 Pour over a mixed greens salad.

# Gazpacho Soup

This soup will definitely get you chilled!

1 Begin by simmering the olive oil with the ganja for about 30 to 45 minutes. Keep the temperature low and try not to burn the weed to ensure a better flavor. I find the taste of the weed can be a bit overpowering so I don't use all of the oil for this first stage, and use the rest to cut the flavor later.

2 Once the oil in finished simmering to extract the THC, the plant matter can be strained out and discarded.

3 Place the tomatoes, celery, onion, bell pepper, garlic and 1 cup of diced tomatoes in a blender and puree.

4 In a large bowl, mix the puree with all the other ingredients and the remaining oil, stirring well to properly combine.

5 Cover the mixture and refrigerate for 2 hours.

6 Divide between 6 bowls and serve cold.

## Ingredients

⅓ cup of olive oil

½ ounce of ground weed

2 large tomatoes, chopped into quarters

2 cans of diced tomatoes

1 cup of green bell pepper, diced

1 onion, diced

2 cloves of garlic, minced

2 small red chilies, de-seeded and chopped

⅓ cup of red wine

1 teaspoon of hot sauce

3 sticks celery, chopped

## Servings

6

## Recommended Dosage

1 bowl

## Preparation Time

20 minutes

## Cooking Time

30 minutes, then 2 hours chilling time

## Chapter 5

# Main Courses

Why restrict your cannabis cuisine to just desserts when you could be enjoying marijuana main meals too? Why not put some Diesel into your Dreamspell Bourbon Barbeque Sauce or some Big Bud into your Bombed Bolognese? These main meal recipes will give you a bigger dose of your favorite medicine along with a huge whack of deliciousness.

# Pothead Pancakes

You'll flip over these pancakes

1 Beat the egg, milk and Marijuana Butter together in a bowl.

2 Mix together the flour, sugar, baking powder and salt together then add to the egg mixture.

3 Pour ⅓ cup of batter into a heated, greased frying pan.

## Ingredients

1 egg

1 ¼ cups of milk

2 tablespoons of Marijuana
   Butter

1 ¼ cups of flour

2 teaspoons of sugar

2 teaspoons of baking
   powder

¼ teaspoon of salt

## Servings

4

## Recommended Dosage

1 serving

## Preparation Time

20 minutes

## Cooking Time

20 minutes

4 When bubbles appear on top of the pancake, flip it and cook for the same amount of time, then serve.

5 Repeat for the rest of the batter, stack the pancakes and drizzle with maple syrup or fruit sauce.

# Grilled Chronic King Salmon

You'll eat like royalty!

1 Season the salmon with salt and pepper and grill until cooked through.

2 Add the white wine, lemon juice and shallots to a heavy-bottomed saucepan and reduce to a syrup.

## Ingredients

4 to 6 grams of hash

4 salmon fillets

1 lemon, sliced

⅛ cup of shallots, chopped

⅛ cup of white wine

⅛ cup of lemon juice

Salt to taste

⅛ cup of heavy cream

½ cup of butter

1 red onion, sliced thinly

½ teaspoon of olive oil

1 pinch of ground cumin

¼ teaspoon of olive oil

¼ red bell pepper, julienned

1 tablespoon of chives,
   chopped

## Servings

4

## Recommended Dosage

1 serving

## Preparation Time

10 minutes

## Cooking Time

24 to 30 minutes

3 Add the heavy cream and the hash.

4 Let it reduce, then slowly add in the butter over a low heat.

5 Strain the sauce and season to taste.

6 In a bowl, mix the fennel, cumin, oil, red pepper, chives, onion and salt together.

7 Sprinkle on top of the salmon steaks and serve everything on a bed of rice, topping it with a slice of lemon.

# Turkey Pot Pies

Gobble one down today!

1 Preheat the oven to 400°F/200°C.

2 Heat the chicken broth and 1 cup of water in a large pan over a high heat. Bring to a boil.

3 Add the turkey and water and cover; reduce heat to low and simmer

## Ingredients

2 cans ready-to-serve
chicken broth

1 cup of water

1 fresh boneless and
skinless turkey breast

3 tablespoons of Marijuana
Butter

1 package of frozen pearl
onions, thawed and
drained

½ teaspoon of sugar

¼ cup of all-purpose flour

2½ cups of milk

½ teaspoon of dried
marjoram, crushed

1 package frozen petite
peas, thawed and
drained

2 cups of carrots, julienned

## Piecrust pastry

1 package shortcrust
pastry

1 egg and 1 tablespoon of
water, beaten together

uncovered for about 25 minutes per pound of
turkey until cooked through.

4 Remove from the broth and let cool.

5 Cut turkey into cubes and set aside.

6 Skim and discard the fat from the broth.

7 Strain the broth and measure 1 cup for
sauce.

8 Melt 1 tablespoon of Marijuana Butter in a

large saucepan. Add the onions and sugar, then reduce heat to medium and sauté for 3 minutes.

9 Remove the onions, and stir the remaining 2 tablespoons of Marijuana Butter and the flour into the saucepan.

10 Cook for 1 to 2 minutes or until mixture is bubbling and slightly golden, stirring constantly.

11 Whisk in the milk and 1 cup of reserved broth; cook until thickened, stirring constantly.

12 Season with marjoram, salt and pepper.

13 Stir in the cubed turkey, onions, peas and carrots and remove from the heat.

14 Roll half the pastry out and cut 6 rounds big enough to cover 6 small aluminum pie dishes.

15 Push the rounds into the dishes.

16 Divide the turkey mixture between the dishes.

17 Roll out the rest of the pastry, creating 6 rounds the same size, and top the pies with the top crust.

18 Pinch the edges of the crusts and trim and excess.

19 Bake for 10 minutes.

20 Reduce the oven temperature to 350°F/175°C and bake for 25 minutes or until the filling is bubbling and the crusts are golden.

**Servings**
6

**Recommended Dosage**
1 pie

**Preparation Time**
35 minutes

**Cooking Time**
35 minutes

# Tacos

Ole!

1 In a large frying pan, sauté the onion and garlic in olive oil. Add in the bud.

2 Add the meat or TVP and brown it with the bud until cooked dry.

3 Add the spices and cook for another 2 minutes.

## Ingredients

1 to 2 grams of ground bud

Hard or soft taco shells

1 pound of lean ground beef (or TVP for a vegetarian option)

2 tablespoons of cumin

2 tablespoons of paprika

1 to 2 tablespoons of chili powder

Chopped jalapeño or chilies (to taste)

1 tomato cut into chunks

1 cup of tomato sauce

1 onion, chopped

1 red pepper, chopped

2 cloves of garlic, crushed

Olive oil

Salt

## Toppings

Shredded lettuce

Shredded cheese

Chopped tomato

## Servings

6

## Recommended Dosage

1 serving

## Preparation Time

15 minutes

## Cooking Time

15 minutes

4 Add in the rest of the ingredients and cook on low, stirring often, until it reaches the desired thickness.

5 Spoon into taco shells and top with lettuce, tomatoes and cheese.

6 Chopped avocado and salsa are also tasty toppings.

# Bud Burger

So good the hamburglar will be after it too.

1 Mix the grated cheese with the chopped bacon and sliced onion and set aside.

2 Combine the hamburger, ground bud, seasoning salt and beer and mix thoroughly, then shape into 6 thin patties.

3 Cook the patties for 14 to 16 minutes on the barbecue until cooked though, flipping midway through cooking

4 Put one patty on a burger bun, top with ⅓ of the cheese mixture, top with another patty and finish with the top of the bun. Repeat for the other burgers and serve.

**Ingredients**

1 ½ grams of ground bud

1 pound of ground beef

6 strips of bacon, crispy

½ red onion, sliced

1 cup of cheddar cheese, grated

½ teaspoon of salt

2 tablespoons of beer

3 burger buns

**Servings**

3

**Recommended Dosage**

1 burger

**Preparation Time**

20 minutes

**Cooking Time**

14 to 16 minutes

# Chicken and Asparagus Fettuccini surprise

Surprise!

1 Cook the fettuccini according to package directions, adding the asparagus during the last 5 minutes of cooking.

2 While the pasta is cooking, heat the butter, Marijuana Butter and cream in a large saucepan over medium heat until both butters are melted and

## Ingredients

2 tablespoons of Marijuana
Butter

12 ounces of dry fettuccini
pasta

2 cups of fresh asparagus,
trimmed and cut into
2½-inch pieces

¼ cup of butter

2 cups of half-and-half

¾ cup of grated Parmesan
cheese

¼ teaspoon of garlic
powder

¼ teaspoon of ground
black pepper

1 pinch of cayenne pepper

½ pound of skinless,
boneless chicken breast,
cooked and cubed

## Servings

4

## Recommended Dosage

1 serving

## Preparation Time

10 minutes

## Cooking Time

15 minutes

the mixture starts to bubble.

3 Stir in the cheese, garlic powder, ground black pepper and cayenne pepper. Continue cooking over medium heat until the mixture is thickened and bubbly.

4 Stir in the chicken.

5 Drain the pasta and asparagus; combine with the sauce and toss to coat evenly. Serve immediately with additional Parmesan cheese, if desired.

# He-man Quiche

This dish is pot-ent!

1 Preheat the oven to 350°F/175°C.

2 Melt the Marijuana Butter in a large skillet over a medium heat, then add the onions and mushrooms and sauté until tender. Remove from the heat, place in a bowl and set aside.

3 Add the sausage to the skillet. Stirring occasionally, sauté until crumbled and cooked through. Drain and stir the onion mixture into the pan with the sausage.

4 Unfold the piecrust and place into a greased, 8-inch round cake pan,

## Ingredients

3 tablespoons of Marijuana Butter, room temperature

2 medium onions, finely chopped

3 cups of fresh mushrooms, chopped

½ pound of hot Italian sausage, casings removed

1 refrigerated folded piecrust

2 cups of shredded Colby-Jack cheese blend

1 ½ cups of heavy cream

3 eggs

## Servings
6

## Recommended Dosage
1 slice

## Preparation Time
15 minutes

## Cooking Time
50 to 55 minutes

pressing firmly against the pan to form a crust.

5 Sprinkle half the cheese over the crust. Alternatively you can split the crust between several aluminum pie dishes to create mini quiches.

6 Top with the sausage mixture, then sprinkle with the remaining cheese.

7 In a medium bowl, whisk together the cream and eggs.

8 Pour over the cheese and sausage, then bake for 50 to 55 minutes, or until a knife inserted in the center comes out clean.

9 Cool for 10 minutes before slicing and serving.

# Dreamspell Bourbon Barbeque Sauce

It'll put you right to sleep.

1 Start by soaking your cannabis in the bourbon for about 24 hours, or as long as possible, in a cool, dark place.

2 After the soaking is done, strain out and discard the plant matter.

## Ingredients

7 grams of bud

1 cup of bourbon

½ can of tomato paste

½ cup of cider vinegar

1 tablespoon of
Worcestershire sauce

2 teaspoons of soy sauce

Juice of 1 lemon

¼ cup of brown sugar

3 cloves garlic, minced

½ onion, minced

½ teaspoon of mustard
seed, crushed (or Dijon)

½ teaspoon of cayenne
pepper

Pinch of salt

## Servings

Makes 1 cup of sauce

## Recommended Dosage

2 to 3 tablespoons

## Preparation Time

Overnight to soak, then
20 minutes

## Cooking Time

20 minutes

3 Combine the ingredients in a heavy-bottomed saucepan and bring to a boil.

4 Allow this mix to simmer for about 20 minutes or until it reaches the desired consistency. Stir occasionally.

5 Cool and mix in a blender for a smoother sauce. Keep refrigerated until ready to use.

# Enchanted Cottage Pie

Fairy tales do come true!

1 Preheat the oven to 350°F/175°C.

2 Boil the potatoes until they're soft and drain them. Mash with the milk and the ½ cup of Marijuana Butter.

3 Melt the 1 tablespoon of Marijuana Butter in a pan and add the onion, carrot and garlic to it. Fry for 5 minutes.

4 Add in the beef and ¼ of the beef stock and cook, stirring, until the meat is browned. Add the rest of the stock and the mushrooms, and season.

5 Cover with a lid and cook for 15 minutes.

6 Sprinkle the flour over the beef mixture and stir until the mixture is thickened.

7 Place the meat mixture into a deep ceramic dish or 4 mini dishes, and cover with the mashed potato. Cook for 30 minutes, until the mashed potato is crisp on top. Serve right away.

## Ingredients

½ cup of Marijuana Butter
+ 1 tablespoon reserve
900 grams of potatoes, peeled and quartered
6 tablespoons of milk
2 cups of ground beef
1 cup of onion, diced
2 cloves of garlic, minced
1 cup of carrot, chopped
2 cups of beef stock
1 cup of button mushrooms, chopped
1 tablespoon of flour

## Servings

1 pie or 4 mini pies

## Recommended Dosage

¼ of the pie, or 1 mini pie

## Preparation Time

30 minutes

## Cooking Time

45 minutes

# Bombed Bolognese

Get Bombed!

1 Melt the Marijuana Butter in a large saucepan, then add the onion and garlic and sauté over a medium heat until the onions are translucent.

2 Add the carrot and celery and sauté for 5 minutes, then add the beef.

## Ingredients

½ cup of Marijuana Butter

1 onion, chopped

3 cloves of garlic, crushed

1 stalk of celery, chopped

2 cups of ground beef

1 can of crushed tomatoes

2 tablespoons of dried
  oregano

1 tablespoon of hot sauce

## Servings

6

## Recommended Dosage

1 serving

## Preparation Time

10 minutes

## Cooking Time

40 minutes

3 When the meat is browned, add the tomatoes, oregano and hot sauce and turn the heat
down.

4 Stir and cook for 30 minutes over a low heat.

5 Serve on top of spaghetti or other pasta, and
top with cheese.

## Chapter 6

# Vegetarian

Whether you're trying to get more veggies into your diet of Cheetos and uncooked brownie mix or you've never touched a plate of beef in your life, you shouldn't have to give up your favorite vice while you give up the meat. These dishes are perfect for a sprinkling of pot, and they're healthier to boot! Double servings, anyone?

# Smashed Pot-atoes

A classic Yu

1 Peel the potatoes if desired, and cube.

2 Place the potatoes in a large saucepan and cover with water.

3 Cook over a medium heat until the potatoes are tender—usually 15 to 20 minutes.

**Ingredients**

5 red potatoes

5 Yukon Gold potatoes

2 tablespoons of Marijuana
Butter

Salt and pepper to taste

½ cup of mayonnaise

½ cup of prepared mustard

½ cup of sour cream

**Servings**

6

**Recommended Dosage**

1 serving with a meal

**Preparation Time**

10 minutes

**Cooking Time**

15 to 20 minutes

**4** Drain and place the cooked potatoes in a large bowl.

**5** Mash the potatoes with the Marijuana Butter, and add salt and pepper to taste.

**6** Once mashed, stir in the mayonnaise, mustard and sour cream, mixing well.

**7** Serve warm or at room temperature.

# Potso Pesto

Buon Appetito e Buona Notta!

1 Begin by simmering ¼ cup of the olive oil with the ganja for about 30 to 45 minutes. Keep the temperature low and try not to burn the weed for a better flavor.

2 Once the oil is finished simmering to extract the THC, the plant matter can be strained out and discarded.

3 Combine all ingredients except the cheese and the majority of the oil in a blender or food processor. Slowly add the rest of the oil while blending on low.

## Ingredients

½ ounce of bud

2 cups of basil leaves

4 cloves of garlic

½ cup of olive oil

½ cup of pine nuts

4 teaspoon of salt

½ cup of Romano cheese

## Servings

4

## Recommended Dosage

1 serving with bread

## Preparation Time

5 minutes

## Cooking Time

45 to 60 minutes

4 Once this mixture is blended to the desired consistency pour it into a bowl and mix in the cheese by hand. Spread over your favorite pasta and enjoy.

**Need an extra kick?**

Place mushrooms caps upside down on a cookie sheet with a bit of garlic and Marijuana Butter in the middle. Broil until golden brown. Add to the top of your pasta dish and garnish with fresh tomatoes and parsley.

# Couscous Your Consciousness

Caution: may induce heightened awareness.

1 Over a medium-low heat, melt the Marijuana Butter in a saucepan.

2 Add the couscous and stir until evenly coated in butter.

3 Add 1 cup of water, bring to a boil, then reduce heat to a simmer.

4 Cover and cook until all the water is absorbed.

5 Set aside to cool.

6 In a salad bowl, combine the couscous, red onion, pepper, parsley, garbanzo beans, almonds and raisins.

7 Stir and mix well.

8 Whisk together the salad dressing, yogurt, cumin, salt and pepper.

9 Drizzle the dressing over the salad and stir until well combined, seasoning with salt and pepper. Chill and serve.

## Ingredients

3 tablespoons of Marijuana Butter

½ cup of couscous

1 red onion, chopped

1 red bell pepper, chopped

⅓ cup of parsley, chopped

⅓ cup of raisins

⅓ cup of toasted, sliced almonds

½ cup of garbanzo beans, drained

½ cup of creamy salad dressing

¼ cup of plain yogurt

1 teaspoon of ground cumin

Salt and pepper to taste

## Servings

6

## Recommended Dosage

1 serving

## Preparation Time

10 minutes

## Cooking Time

10 to 15 minutes

# Carrot Casserole

Always a grate choice.

1 Preheat oven to 325°F/160°C.

2 Grease a 1-quart casserole dish or 6 mini casserole dishes.

3 In a large mixing bowl, combine the cooked carrots and the Marijuana Butter and stir well.

4 Mix in the sugar, milk, salt, cinnamon, nutmeg, eggs and vanilla extract.

5 Pour into the casserole dish/es.

6 Bake for 20 to 30 minutes, or 10 to 15 minutes for mini casseroles, just until set. Serve.

## Ingredients

2 cups of mashed, cooked carrots

3 to 4 tablespoons of Marijuana Butter

1 cup of white sugar

⅓ cup of milk

½ teaspoon of salt

1 teaspoon of ground cinnamon

1 teaspoon of ground nutmeg

3 eggs

1 teaspoon of vanilla extract

## Servings

6

## Recommended Dosage

⅙ of the casserole, or 1 mini casserole

## Preparation Time

10 minutes

## Cooking Time

45 minutes

# Corny Casserole

You'll niblet all night long!

1 Preheat oven to 350°F/175°C.

2 In a medium bowl, cream together the Marijuana Butter and cream cheese.

3 Mix in the whole-kernel corn, the cream-style corn, chilies, chopped onions and ½ can of the French-fried onions.

4 Pour the mixture into a 1-quart casserole dish or 8 mini dishes.

5 Bake for 15 minutes, or 10 minutes for the mini casseroles.

6 Remove from the oven and sprinkle the remaining French-fried onions over the top of the casserole.

7 Return to the oven and bake for an additional 15 minutes, or 10 minutes for the mini casseroles.

## Ingredients

⅓ cup of Marijuana Butter

2 (3 ounce) packages of cream cheese

1 can of whole-kernel corn, drained

1 can of cream-style corn

1 can of chopped green chilies

½ cup of onion, chopped

1 can of French-fried onions

## Servings

8

## Recommended Dosage

⅛ serving of the casserole, or 1 mini casserole

## Preparation Time

5 minutes

## Cooking Time

30 minutes

# Primeval Pasta

Get back to the stoned age!

1 Cook the pasta in boiling water for 10 minutes or until it's done, then drain.

2 Melt the butter and Marijuana Butter over a medium heat in a large saucepan.

3 Sauté the onions, mushrooms and garlic until tender.

## Ingredients

2 tablespoons of Marijuana
  Butter

1 package of rotini

2 tablespoons of butter

3 cloves of garlic, crushed

2 cups of mushrooms,
  sliced

1 medium onion, chopped

10 ounces of marinated
  artichoke hearts

1 cup of sun-dried
  tomatoes, packed in oil

½ cup of black olives,
  sliced

1 teaspoon of black pepper

1 ripe tomato, chopped

2 tablespoons of lemon
  juice

1 cup of dry white wine

1 cup of Parmesan cheese

## Servings

4

## Recommended Dosage

1 serving

## Preparation Time

10 minutes

## Cooking Time

20 minutes

4 Stir in sun-dried tomatoes, olives, artichoke hearts, wine and lemon juice.

5 Bring to a boil and cook until the liquid is reduced by about a third. This should take about 4 minutes.

6 Top with tomatoes and cheese, season and serve.

# Veg-Out Stoner Pie

The perfect meal for all couch potatoes.

1 Preheat oven to 350°F/175°C.

2 Gently boil the potatoes in a large pot of water for 20 minutes, or until tender. Drain and return to the pot.

3 Mash the potatoes with the 3 tablespoons of Marijuana Butter, 3/4 tea-

## Ingredients

3 tablespoons of Marijuana
  Butter

5 russet potatoes, peeled
  and cut into chunks

2 tablespoons of butter

1 ½ teaspoon of salt

Ground black pepper

2 cups of milk

3 cups of water

½ cup of kasha

2 tablespoons of butter

2 cups of chopped onion

2 cloves of garlic, minced

2 carrots, diced

2 cups of fresh mushrooms,
  sliced

1 ½ tablespoons of all-
  purpose flour

1 cup of whole-kernel corn,
  blanched

3 tablespoons of fresh
  parsley, chopped

spoon of salt and ½ cup of milk until fairly
smooth, then set aside.

4 In a saucepan, bring 1 ½ cups of water with
½ teaspoon of salt to the boil.

5 Stir in the kasha, reduce the heat and simmor,
uncovered, for 15 minutes.

6 Add 1 ½ cups more water and bring to a boil.

7 Cover and remove from the heat. Let stand

for 10 minutes.

**8** In a large saucepan, melt 2 tablespoons of butter over a medium heat.

**9** Add the onions, garlic and carrots and sauté until the onions soften.

**10** Add the mushrooms and cook and stir for 3 to 4 minutes.

**11** Sprinkle the flour over the vegetables and stir for 2 minutes.

**12** Pour the remaining 1 $\frac{1}{2}$ cups of milk over the vegetables and increase the heat to high.

**13** Stir with a whisk until the sauce is smooth.

**14** Reduce the heat and simmer for 5 minutes.

**15** Stir in the corn, $\frac{1}{4}$ teaspoon of salt and black pepper to taste.

**16** Mix together the vegetable mixture and kasha mixture.

**17** Spoon into a buttered 10-inch pie pan, and smooth with a spatula.

**18** Spread mashed potatoes over the top, leaving an uneven surface.

**19** Bake for 30 minutes.

**20** Garnish with the chopped parsley and serve.

**Servings**

4 to 6

**Recommended Dosage**

$\frac{1}{4}$ or $\frac{1}{8}$ of the pie

**Preparation Time**

20 minutes

**Cooking Time**

1 hour and 45 minutes

# Veggie Chili

A hearty meal that will leaf you wanting more!

1 Soak the lentils in boiling water for 30 minutes, then drain and rinse.

2 Fry the onion, garlic, chili powder, cumin and paprika and the melted Marijuana Butter.

3 Add the pepper, carrots and lentils and cook for 5 minutes.

## Ingredients

3 tablespoons of Marijuana Butter

1 cup of red lentils

1 large onion, chopped

2 cloves of garlic, crushed

2 teaspoons of chili powder

1 teaspoon of cumin

1 teaspoon of paprika

1 red bell pepper, chopped

400 grams of chopped tomatoes

1 tablespoon of tomato puree

1 cup of vegetable stock

1 cup of frozen peas

2 carrots, chopped

2 cups of mushrooms, chopped

1 can of kidney beans, drained

## Servings

4 to 6

## Recommended Dosage

1 serving

## Preparation Time

30 minutes

## Cooking Time

40 minutes

4 Add the tomatoes, puree, stock and peas, bring to a boil then turn down and simmer for 30 minutes.

5 Add the mushrooms and simmer for 5 minutes.

6 Add the kidney beans and simmer for 5 minutes

7 Serve with rice and a slice of lime.

## Chapter 7

# More Desserts

It is a truth, universally acknowledged, that a person can never have enough dessert. This is especially true for stoners; that second brownie is never quite enough when you're high as a kite with cut strings. Desserts are also really useful if you overindulge a little (yes you, at the back, you know who I'm talking about) as the sugar content can help bring you back to reality a little. If you feel yourself on the verge of a white out, a glass of orange and an oatmeal cookie will work magic!

# Going Bananas

A peel-good recipe.

**1** In a large, deep skillet, melt the Marijuana Butter and butter over a medium heat.
**2** Stir in the sugar, rum, vanilla and cinnamon.
**3** When the mixture begins to bubble, place the bananas and walnuts in a pan.
**4** Cook until the bananas are hot; about 1 to 2 minutes.
**5** Serve at once over vanilla ice cream

## Ingredients

2 tablespoons of Marijuana Butter
1 ¼ cup of butter
⅔ cup of dark brown sugar
3 ½ tablespoons of rum
1 ½ teaspoons of vanilla extract
½ teaspoon of ground cinnamon
3 bananas, peeled and sliced
½ cup of walnuts, coarsely chopped
1 pint of vanilla ice cream

## Servings

4

## Recommended Dosage

1 serving

## Preparation Time

3 minutes

## Cooking Time

4 minutes

# Fruit Salad

Orange you glad you tried this?

1 Dissolve the ginger in the brandy tincture.
2 Combine the oranges, pineapple cubes and
grapes in a bowl.
3 Pour the brandy over the fruits, basting them
for a few moments.
4 Cover the bowl and chill for 3 hours. Arrange
the salad on lettuce leaves in bowls and serve.

Note: You can use other fruit and / or melon
combinations with this brandy dressing but the
pineapple soaks up a lot of brandy.

**Ingredients**

½ cup of brandy tincture

2 teaspoons of powdered
  ginger

2 oranges, peeled and
  thinly sliced

1 cup of fresh or canned
  pineapple cubes

1 cup of grapes

**Servings**

2

**Recommended Dosage**

1 serving

**Preparation Time**

20 minutes to prepare,
3 hours to chill

# Skunky Shortbread

A shortbread but a long high!

**1** Preheat oven to 325°F/160°C.

**2** Mix the flour and sugar together in a bowl.

**3** Chop the Marijuana Butter in small chunks and add it to the bowl.

**4** Rub the Marijuana Butter into the flour mixture until you get a crumbly mixture that stays together when pressed.

**5** Add the vanilla extract and work to distribute evenly.

**6** Press the dough into a greased baking pan (something like an 8 x 8-inch pan) and bake for 30 minutes.

**7** Cut, cool and enjoy!

**Ingredients**

½ cup of Marijuana Butter, room temperature

1 ¼ cups of flour

⅓ cup of sugar

1 teaspoon of vanilla extract

**Servings**

24 pieces

**Recommended Dosage**

2 to 3 pieces

**Preparation Time**

10 minutes

**Cooking Time**

30 minutes

# Decadent Chocolate Bud Cake

Perfect for you and your buds.

1 Preheat oven to 350°F/175°C.

2 Grease two or three 9-inch round cake pans.

3 In a medium bowl, pour boiling water over the cocoa and whisk until smooth. Set aside to cool.

4 Sift together the flour, baking soda, baking powder and salt and set aside.

## Ingredients

2 tablespoons of Marijuana
   Butter

²/₃ cup of boiling water

⅓ cup of unsweetened
   cocoa powder

³/₄ cup and 2 tablespoons
   of all-purpose flour

¼ teaspoon of baking soda

⅛ teaspoon of baking
   powder

⅛ teaspoon of salt

⅓ cup of butter, softened

³/₄ cup of white sugar

1 ⅓ eggs

½ teaspoons of vanilla
   extract

## Servings

4

## Recommended Dosage

1 serving

Preparation Time

10 minutes

## Cooking Time

25 to 30 minutes

5 In a large bowl, cream together the butter,
Marijuana Butter and sugar until light and fluffy.

6 Beat in the eggs one at a time, then stir in the
vanilla extract.

7 Add the flour mixture and the cocoa mixture
alternately, then stir to combine.

8 Spread the batter evenly between the prepared pans.

9 Bake for 25 to 30 minutes, then set aside to
cool.

10 Decorate with chocolate butter cream or
your favorite frosting and enjoy!

# Shiva's Chai Cupcakes

You'll wish that you "chai-ed" these before!

**1** Preheat oven to 350°F/175°C and line a cupcake tin with cupcake wrappers.

**2** Heat the milk in a pan until it's almost boiling, then remove from the heat and throw in the 2 chai tea bags. Allow to sit for 10 minutes.

**3** Remove the tea bags from the milk and stir in the apple cider vinegar.

**4** In a bowl, sift together the flour, icing sugar, baking soda, cinnamon,

## Ingredients

⅓ cup of Marijuana Butter, melted

2 cups of all-purpose flour

1 cup of powdered sugar

2 teaspoons of baking soda

1½ cups of almond milk

2 good quality chai tea bags

1 tablespoon of apple cider vinegar

2 teaspoons of vanilla extract

1 teaspoon of ground cinnamon

1 teaspoon of ground ginger

½ teaspoon of ground nutmeg

## Servings

12 cupcakes

## Recommended Dosage

1 cupcake

## Preparation Time

20 minutes

## Cooking Time

20 minutes

ginger and nutmeg.

5 Stir the melted Marijuana Butter and vanilla extract into the milk mixture, then combine the milk mixture with the flour mixture. Stir until just combined.

6 Divide between the cupcake wrappers and bake for 20 minutes.

7 Allow to cool, then frost with your favorite frosting—a vanilla cinnamon buttercream works great!

# Baked Apple Crumble

## You'll be truly baked!

1 Preheat oven to 350°F/175°C.

2 In a bowl, combine the brown sugar, oats, flour and melted Marijuana Butter. Rub the mixture together with your fingers until it resembles breadcrumbs.

3 Combine the apples, white sugar and cinnamon in a separate bowl and stir to combine.

4 Place the apple mixture in the bottom of a ceramic dish, or divide between 4 smaller dishes.

5 Top with the crumble and bake for 40 to 50 minutes, until the top is golden brown.

**Ingredients**

½ cup of Marijuana Butter, melted

1 cup of brown sugar

1 cup of rolled oats

1 cup of all-purpose flour

3 cups of apples, peeled, cored and chopped

½ cup of white sugar

2 teaspoons of ground cinnamon

**Servings**

1 large crumble or 4 mini crumbles

**Recommended Dosage**

1 mini crumble or ¼ of a large crumble

**Preparation Time**

20 minutes

**Cooking Time**

20 minutes

## Chapter 8

# Marijuana Drinks

Over the last several years, flavored alcohol has become very popular and since cannabinoids dissolve well in alcohol, it's easy and worthwhile to make marijuana alcohol. Generally, for this purpose, the stronger the alcohol content, the better. Grain alcohol is pure alcohol–odorless, tasteless and very potent. At 190 proof, grain alcohol makes an extremely strong brew that I recommend only to be used in moderation. Instead, I prefer to use vodka. Most midlevel vodkas are now triple-filtered and this helps to make them purer. Fewer impurities mean less of a hangover.

The alcoholic cocktail and shots recipes use the basic Marijuana Extraction Method on page 20. I'd recommend 1 of these cocktails and 2 at the maximum. After that, switch to something softer!

# Dirty Bong Water

1 ounce Of Chambord Raspberry Liqueur

1 ounce of Malibu Coconut Rum

Splash of sweet & sour mix

Splash of pineapple juice

½ ounce of blue curaçao

½ gram of ground bud

**Directions:**

Mix well. Makes 2 shots.

# Motherfucker

This one doesn't need any weed!

½ ounce of absinthe

1 ounce of rum

**Directions:**

Mix well.

# Vlad the Inhaler's Vodka

1 ounce of Marijuana Vodka

½ ounce of gin

½ ounce of light rum

½ ounce of tequila

2 dashes of cola so you can see when you get to
   the bottom of the glass.

Juice of ½ lemon

**Directions:**

Combine the ingredients

and pour over ice in a

highball glass.

Garnish with a slice of lemon.

# Mary Jane's Martini

2 ounces of Marijuana Vodka

1 ½ ounces of Apple Barrel
    Schnapps

3 drops of Midori

**Directions:**

Shake with ice and strain.

Garnish with a slice of
    green apple and enjoy!

# Ghetto Booty

½ ounce of raspberry vodka

½ ounce of Grand Marnier Orange
   Liqueur

¼ gram of ground bud

**Directions:**

Mix well.

# Bourbon High

2 ounces of bourbon

Ginger ale or club soda

½ gram of ground bud

**Directions:**

Fill highball glass with bourbon,

   ginger ale or club soda and ice

   cubes. Add in the bud.

Add ice and twist of lemon peel, if

   desired, and stir.

# Indian Summer

1 ounce of amaretto

½ ounce of vodka

½ ounce of Kahlua

½ gram of ground bud

**Directions:**

Mix well. Makes 2 shots.

# Surfer
# on Acid

½ ounce of Jägermeister

½ ounce of Malibu Rum

½ ounce of pineapple juice

½ gram of ground bud

**Directions:**

Shake over ice.

# Freight Train

1 ounce of Jack Daniels

1 ounce of tequila

$3/4$ gram of ground bud

**Directions:**

Shake, no ice.

# Sangria

Smashing sangria for the girly-man in all of us.

4 shots of Marijuana Brandy

1 bottle of red wine

1 lemon, cut into wedges

1 orange, cut into wedges

2 tablespoons of sugar

2 cups of ginger ale or club soda

**Directions**

Mix the sugar into the wine.

Add the lemon, orange and any

other fruit you desire, Marijuana

Brandy and club soda or

ginger ale.

Add ice to chill.

Stir and serve.

**Servings**

4

**Recommended Dosage**

4 to 6 servings

**Preparation Time**

10 minutes

# Coffee Chai

Your klatch will be staggering.

1 Place the milk and honey into a pan over a medium heat and cook until almost boiling.

2 Add the marijuana and simmer at a low heat for at least half an hour.

3 Strain the milk through a cheesecloth and discard the marijuana.

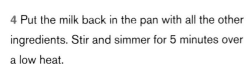

### Ingredients

4 cups of milk

1 tablespoon of honey

2 grams of finely chopped
  marijuana

1 tablespoon of instant or
  freeze-dried coffee

¼ cup of brown sugar

3 cinnamon sticks

6 cardamom pods

⅛ teaspoon of grated
  nutmeg

⅛ teaspoon of allspice

4 cinnamon sticks, optional

### Servings

4

### Recommended Dosage

1 cup

### Preparation Time

30 minutes

### Cooking Time

30 minutes

4 Put the milk back in the pan with all the other ingredients. Stir and simmer for 5 minutes over a low heat.

5 Remove from the heat and sit for 20 minutes.

6 Pour through a clean sieve and serve!

# Bhang Lassi

Spice up your life!

1 Quickly rinse the plant matter in cold water. This is believed to prevent headaches sometimes experienced from ingesting bhang.

2 Next, boil the water and pour it into a clean pot.

3 Add the dry ingredients and allow it to steep for about 7 minutes.

4 Strain the liquid through a muslin cloth; as much water as possible should be squeezed out.  Set liquid aside.

5 Crush the bud and spices with 2 tablespoons of warm milk in a pestle and mortar and mash into a paste.

6 Strain off the milk and repeat Step 5 until about 1 cup of milk has been used.

7 Trash the bud and spices and keep the milk.

8 Combine the milk with the rosewater and the initial tea and add honey to taste. Chill and enjoy!

For a much quicker and easier method, try simmering the dry ingredients with 1 to 2 cups of milk for 30 minutes or more; longer is better. Strain this mixture and cool. Add 2 cups of yogurt and some honey and voila! Your day is set.

**Ingredients**

1 gram of ground bud

2 cups of water

4 cups of warm milk

3 tablespoons of chopped almonds

½ teaspoon of cinnamon

Pinch of nutmeg

Pinch of cardamom

Pinch of caraway

½ tablespoon of poppy seeds

½ tablespoon of chopped ginger

1 teaspoon of rosewater

Honey to taste

**Servings**

4 to 6

**Recommended Dosage**

1 glass

**Preparation Time**

15 minutes

**Cooking Time**

10 minutes

# Pot Chocolate

Don't forget the marshmallows!

1 Put the milk, chocolate, 2 cinnamon sticks and the weed into a heavy-bottomed saucepan and bring it to a boil. Milk burns easily, so stir constantly.

2 Once the mixture is boiling, reduce the heat and simmer for about 5 minutes.

**Ingredients**

1 gram of ground bud

1 cup of milk / soy milk

4 ounces of semisweet
    chocolate

6 cinnamon sticks

Sugar or honey

**Servings**

4

**Recommended Dosage**

1 cup

**Preparation Time**

5 minutes

**Cooking Time**

8 minutes

3 Remove from the heat and strain.

4 Pour into cups and garnish with a cinnamon stick for stirring.

5 Sweeten to taste, then serve.

# Cappuccino Chill Out

Chillax yourself!

1 Put the milk and weed into a heavy-bottomed saucepan and heat gently, stirring often, for 1 hour.

2 Strain the plant matter from the milk and allow it to cool.

3 Stir the sugar and coffee into the marijuana milk until the coffee is dissolved, then pour it into a 13 x 9-inch baking pan.

4 Cover loosely with plastic wrap and freeze overnight.

5 To serve, scrape with a spoon or ice cream scoop.

6 Place in a glass and sprinkle with cinnamon.

**Ingredients**

2 to 3 grams of bud, ground

4 cups of milk

2 tablespoons of instant espresso or coffee crystals

6 tablespoons of sugar

Cinnamon for garnish

**Servings**

4

**Recommended Dosage**

1 glass

**Preparation Time**

5 minutes

**Cooking Time**

1 hour, with resting overnight

# Stir-Crazy Shake

It'll have you looking beyond the stars!

1 Put the milk and weed into a heavy-bottomed saucepan and heat gently, stirring often, for 1 hour.

2 Strain the plant matter from the milk and allow it to cool.

3 Stir all the ingredients together or quickly blend them, then divide between 3 glasses and serve.

**Ingredients**

2 grams of bud, ground

3 cups of milk

3 scoops of vanilla ice cream

3 tablespoons of chocolate topping

**Servings**

3

**Recommended Dosage**

1 glass

**Preparation Time**

5 minutes

**Cooking Time**

1 hour

# Spaced-Out Banana Shake

You'll be in a different galaxy!

1 Put the milk and weed into a heavy-bottomed saucepan and heat gently, stirring often, for 1 hour.
2 Strain the plant matter from the milk and allow it to cool.

**Ingredients**

2 grams of bud, ground

2 cups of milk

1 large scoop of ice cream

3 small bananas

1 apple, peeled and cored

**Servings**

3

**Recommended Dosage**

1 glass

**Preparation Time**

5 minutes

**Cooking Time**

1 hour

3 Pour the milk, ice cream, bananas and apple into a blender and pulse for 30 seconds.

4 Serve with crushed nuts on top.

## Chapter 9

# Eat, Drink and Detoxify

## Kenn A. Biscranium

Drug testing is an unfortunate fact of life for many people. A worse fact is that few people know how to properly "study" for a drug test. When I say study, I mean eating the correct foods and drinking the right teas so that

if you are ever told to provide a urine sample for a drug test, you'll be able to pass. But before I list what foods to eat, which amino acids are needed, and how to make detox tea, I need to give you the basics of how the body's detoxification system works.

The human body changes all fat-soluble toxins to water-soluble toxins prior to excreting them. Therefore, stop believing that THC takes long periods of time to be eliminated from the body simply because THC is fat-soluble. (In this writing, when I refer to THC, I am referring to THC or THC metabolites.) The truth is that THC is quickly converted into a water-soluble toxin and rapidly eliminated when you eat the correct foods. And drink water. Lots of water. Liters and liters a day.

The liver is the organ that does most, if not all, of the body's detoxification. (The skin, lungs, and kidneys do help with detox a bit.) The liver is

vital to the body's circulatory system; it filters the blood. The liver catches the toxins from your blood, eliminates them, and keeps you healthy. At the same time, the liver is vital to the body's digestive system; it produces bile (which is stored in the gallbladder), metabolizes fat, and conjugates (changes) toxins for excretion from the body.

No organ in the body is more important than the liver. No organ in the body is larger than the liver—proof that size is important.

Another fact that emphasizes the importance of the liver to the body: the liver is one of the few parts of the body that will regenerate cells. The liver can actually repair itself after it has been injured, by growing new cells. More amazing, even if more than a majority of the liver was damaged from toxins, pesticides, or ingested metals it will still regenerate cells and be as good as new in a few weeks. (This is not inclusive of cirrhosis, cancer, or other diseases.) Keep your liver strong and healthy with the proper diet and you will be able to detox THC quickly – and pass a UA today type of drug test.

## Cut to the Chase

There are two phases of the body's detoxification system: phase 1 and phase 2. These phases are sometimes referred to as pathways.

Phase 1 is known as the cytochrome P450 enzyme system. This is where the liver cells (Hepatocytes) take the toxins, and through various chemical reactions known as oxidation, reduction, and hydrolysis turn the toxins into a less harmful substance. During these chemical reactions free radicals are generated. To prevent cellular damage, there is an important need for antioxidants, especially vitamin C.

To enhance the strength and effectiveness of the phase 1 cytochrome P450 enzyme system, eat more:

- Garlic
- Onions
- Artichokes
- Beets
- Natural carotenoids (carrots, sweet potatoes, mangoes, pumpkin)
- All kinds of berries (blue, black, rasp, straw)

- Glutathione (asparagus, spinach, avocados, papaya)
- Choline (milk, eggs, peanuts, wheat germ)
- Copper (shellfish, nuts, lima beans, peas, lentils)
- Iron (meat, wheat germ, oats, fortified cereal)
- Magnesium (lima beans, broccoli, artichokes, yogurt)
- Manganese (pineapples, nuts, leafy green vegetables)
- Molybdenum (peas, leafy green vegetables, cruciferous vegetables, oats)
- Selenium (seafood, meat, fortified cereal)
- Zinc (oysters, legumes, pumpkin seeds, wheat germ)
- Riboflavin, vitamin B2, sometimes called vitamin G (milk, cheese, leafy green vegetables, almonds)
- Niacin, vitamin B3 (meat, poultry, figs, prunes, brown rice) Note: There are two types of Niacin. Niacinamide and Nicotinic Acid. For flushing out the capillaries, make sure you're taking Nicotinic Acid.
- Pyridoxine, vitamin B6 (tuna, bananas, bell peppers, spinach)
- Cobalamin, vitamin B12 (meat, poultry, milk, eggs)
- Ascorbic Acid, vitamin C (citrus fruits, strawberries, kiwi, broccoli, bell peppers, guava) Vitamin E (eggs, almonds, wheat germ, spinach, avocado)

Phase 2 is also known as the conjugation pathway. The Hepatocytes add either a glycine or sulphate molecule to a toxin to make it water-soluble. It can then be eliminated from the body in a fluid such as urine or bile. In order to pass a drug test, you must strengthen the effectiveness of your phase 2 to conjugate those toxins to water-soluble and eliminate them from the body. Here is a list of what you need to eat more of:

- Garlic
- Onions
- Cruciferous vegetables (cabbage, broccoli, cauliflower, brussels sprouts, kale)
- Glutamine (meat, fish, beans, dairy products)
- Glycine (meat, fish, beans, dairy products)
- Cysteine (red peppers, cruciferous vegetables, oats, milk, wheat germ) Glucarate (apples, cruciferous vegetables, bean sprouts)

If you might have to take a drug test, stop eating fried, deep-fried, and fatty foods. Stop eating processed foods and foods with added chemicals. Also, stop eating smoked, cured, and salted meats. Eat much more fruits and vegetables, especially the ones on the two lists given above.

## Finding the WMD (Way of Mucho Detox)

It's not so much THC being fat-soluble that keeps it in your body for so long, it's the fact that marijuana contains the two drugs, cannabinol (CBN) and cannabidiol (CBD). These two drugs slow down the liver and prevent the detoxification process from happening. CBN and CBD prevent the production of the cytochrome P450 enzymes. When you ingest pot, you're taking drugs that signal your body's detox system (both phases) to slow down and not metabolize THC. This is the main reason why it takes so long to metabolize THC: you're taking drugs that tell your body not to eliminate drugs.

What is a stoner looking for a job or a pothead on parole going to do? Maybe consider no more ingesting of marijuana? Nah, that choice sucks. But there are polyphenols. Polyphenols are what you need to ensure that your detox system is not slowed down by CBN and CBD. Polyphenols from caffeinated tea work the best. When I say tea, I mean real tea from the Camellia sinensis plant (green, black, white, or oolong), not the infusion I describe later in this chapter that most everyone in America, myself included, calls "tea."

If you are facing the possibility of random drug tests, and you want to continue enjoying marijuana, you must overpower the effects of cannabinol and cannabidiol with the polyphenols in caffeinated tea. It's as simple as that. But if you drink a couple cups of tea a day, each and every day, then eat seaweed once in a while to offset any excess fluorine.

## Spicy Meets Balls

You have probably already noticed that garlic and onions made it onto both lists of what to eat to help each phase of the detoxification system. (Antonio, your momma would be so happy.) It's the sulphurated phytochemicals that make garlic so helpful, and to a lesser degree, onions also. And there are other spices that you should be adding to your food every day if you might have to submit to a random drug test.

## CAYENNE PEPPER

Start with cayenne pepper. No other spice is as helpful as this one. Cayenne pepper improves blood circulation and is effective at removing any THC that is trapped deep inside fat tissue. Cayenne helps makes it possible to metabolize all the THC and eliminate it from the body. Add cayenne pepper to your recipes to help pass drug tests.

Additionally, cayenne pepper makes all the other spices and foods you're eating for detox work much better. For example, garlic helps both phases of your detox system, but garlic and cayenne kicks ass for detoxification.

## TURMERIC

Turmeric's active ingredient is curcumin, a polyphenol. Turmeric strengthens the liver, induces the flow of bile, and cleans toxins from the body.

## BURDOCK ROOT

Burdock root is excellent for cleaning the blood and detoxing the liver. It has been used for centuries as a blood cleanser. It also induces the flow of bile.

## MILK THISTLE

Milk thistle strengthens the liver and is a powerful antioxidant. It's an excellent enhancer for the regeneration of liver cells. Milk thistle has flavonoid-like compounds called flavonolignans, the group of which is collectively called silymarin.

## DANDELION

Dandelion could be called a superdetoxifier in that it stimulates the elimination of toxins from every cell in the body. Dandelion contains choline, which increases bile production and stimulates its flow to the gallbladder.

## GINGER

Ginger stimulates the vasomotor and respiratory systems as well as stimulating blood circulation. It aids digestion, and when combined with other herbs, ginger enhances their effectiveness (much like cayenne pepper).

## ALFALFA

Alfalfa, also known as lucerne, is excellent for detoxification. Its leaves contain flavones, isoflavones, sterols, and coumarin derivatives.

## LICORICE ROOT

Licorice root cleanses the colon and enhances microcirculation in the gastrointestinal lining.

## FENNEL SEED

Fennel seed promotes good digestion by increasing production of bile. It also helps to break down fats.

## FENUGREEK SEED

Fenugreek seed stimulates perspiration and helps remove toxins from the respiratory tract.

## HIBISCUS

Hibiscus is a mild blood and digestive system cleaner.

You should be adding these spices and herbs to your food regularly if you want to pass your drug tests. The more of these spices you put in

your food, the more effective they will be at cleaning toxins out of your system.

## They're Called Essential for a Good Reason

If you don't regularly take in enough of the right vitamins you will get sick. You will get diseases. And you will die. Luckily for us, in today's world most foods are fortified with vitamins, so we don't have to concern ourselves with vitamin deficiency.

But just because today's foods are fortified to prevent malnutrition doesn't mean you're getting enough vitamins for detoxification — especially vitamin C.

Vitamin C is absolutely essential for detoxification. Vitamin C is an electron donor and it attaches to the toxin in order for the toxin to be eliminated. Without vitamin C to "fuel" your detox system, you won't be getting rid of toxins as quickly as possible. Without vitamin C, your detox system runs out of fuel and remains idle. Without plenty of vitamin C, toxins will stay in the body. That's not good.

You should be eating fruits and vegetables that have significant amounts of vitamin C every day — except for grapefruit. During your detoxification, do not eat any grapefruit. Grapefruits contain a chemical called narangin. The chemical narangin interferes with the cytochrome P450 enzymes.

In addition to all the fruits and vegetable you will now be eating that are loaded with vitamin C, eat vitamin C chewables. The recommended daily allowance (RDA) for vitamin C is 60mg. For detox, you should be eating at least 3,000mg a day, divided up throughout the day.

It's difficult to take too much vitamin C since it's a water-soluble vitamin. And due to the fact that vitamin C keeps detoxification happening in your body, each and every day you need to eat thousands of milligrams of vitamin C.

Vitamin A – Is a powerful antioxidant and is helpful for keeping the inside of the body clean. It is a fat-soluble vitamin. A person could take too much of vitamin A and should not take more than 5,000 International Units (I.U.) in a single day. Although the retinoids and carotenoids are

nontoxic, and you cannot eat too much of those.

Vitamin B – The entire B-complex group is beneficial for detoxification. In one way or another, all eight B vitamins help keep the metabolism, digestive system, and circulatory system running in top condition.

Many people already know that taking megadoses (500-1,000 mg) of Niacin is an excellent way to flush out THC from the body. Megadoses of Niacin are able to remove THC by opening the capillaries and allowing toxins that are deep inside your body to move into the circulatory system, get metabolized, then excreted.

Do not flush with Niacin the day of your drug test. Also, do not take Niacinamide and expect to get the "Niacin flush." You must take mega doses of Nicotinic Acid to open the capillaries.

Niacinamide is a synthetic vitamin. It is manufactured to be time-re-

leased in the body in order to specifically not give the Niacin flush. This synthetic, time-released form of Vitamin B3 is made because opening the capillaries with large dosage of Nicotinic Acid will give a person hot flashes, lightheadedness, and brief moments of dizziness. And as odd as it may sound, some people prefer not to have that happen.

All B Vitamins are water-soluble and therefore, it is difficult to take too much and suffer any long-term consequences. Also, taking Vitamin B is how to get some color in your urine sample if you plan on drinking lots of water before a UA.

Vitamin E – Is another powerful antioxidant and is helpful for improved blood circulation. It is also a fat-soluble vitamin and a person should not take too more than 400 I.U. in a single day.

## "Water To Think, Water To Drink, Water Over Me"

For those who don't recognize that, it's a line from a Peter Gabriel song. And for those who don't realize it, water is life. No animal or plant survives without water. Seventy-five percent of the human body is water.

Scientifically, water is known as the universal solvent. And from science class I'm sure you remember that a solvent is a fluid (liquid, gas, or plasma) that dissolves a solid or gaseous solute, resulting in a solution.

Water is crucial both as a solvent for dissolving many of the body's solutes and as an essential component of many metabolic processes within the body. No other single substance is as important for our health.

Water is just as important for detoxification as it is for sustaining life and health. Without plenty of clean water you cannot detox. Think about it: you rely on water to wash and rinse everything…to take a shower, wash your car, brush your teeth, clean your dishes, do your laundry. You can't do any of these without water.

Detox is no different. For detoxification of drug metabolites you must be cleaning and rinsing the inside of your body by drinking plenty of clean filtered water. If you drink water that has traces of chemicals in it, you're forcing your liver to work harder to eliminate those chemicals, instead of working to eliminate THC.

Drinking plenty of water means 7, 8, 9, maybe even 10 glasses of water a day. And if you smoke weed during a period of time in which you might have to take a random drug test, drink more water than that. Every day. The first thing to do when you wake up is drink a big glass of water. It's the healthiest habit you can practice for yourself. Your body has dehydrated throughout the night simply by you breathing. So you're dehydrated just from that, you urinate, then most of you drink a cup of coffee (the caffeine is a diuretic); you are in need of a lot of water just to start your day!

Water throughout the day and a glass of water before each meal is a must. It is a healthier habit for more efficient digestion if you drink all the fluids before you begin eating. You'll eat less and you won't dilute the digestive enzymes.

For detoxification, you must be drinking many glasses of water each day. Water is the only way to wash away toxins once you've turned them water-soluble.

## Detox Tea Recipe

Start by boiling 2 quarts of filtered water. Once the water starts to boil, remove from heat and let sit for 5 minutes. Then add:

2 cups of burdock root

1 cup of milk thistle

1 cup of red clover

1 cup of dandelion

½ cup of licorice root

Let steep for 25 minutes. Strain all ingredients. Drink, enjoy, and detoxify.

---

Kenn A. Biscranium is the author of *Passing Drug Tests,* the humorous book that explains Kenn's episodes of being on parole, smoking weed just about every day, and what he did to pass all the random UAs. It's available at http://www.uadetox.com or www.uadetox.com.

# Scheduling Definitions

**Scheduling definitions established by The Controlled Substances Act of 1970**

## SCHEDULE I
### Includes heroin, LSD, and marijuana

A The drug or other substance has a high potential for abuse.

B The drug or other substance has no currently accepted medical use in treatment in the United States.

C There is a lack of accepted safety for the use of the drug or other substance under medical supervision.

## SCHEDULE II
### Includes Marinol, methadone, morphine, methamphetamine, and cocaine

A The drug or other substance has a high potential for abuse.

B The drug or other substance has a currently accepted medical use in treatment in the United States or a currently accepted medical use with severe restrictions.

C Abuse of the drug or other substances may lead to severe psychological or physical dependence.

## SCHEDULE III
### Includes anabolic steroids

A The drug or other substance has a potential of abuse less than the drugs or other substances in Schedules I and II.

B The drug or other substance has a currently accepted medical use in treatment in the United States.

C Abuse of the drug or other substance may lead to moderate or low physical dependence or high psychological dependence.

# SCHEDULE IV
## Includes Valium and other tranquilizers

A The drug or other substance has a low potential for abuse relative to the drugs or other substances in Schedule III.

B The drug or other substance has a currently accepted medical use in treatment in the United States.

C Abuse of the drug or other substance may lead to limited physical dependence or psychological dependence relative to the drugs or other substances in Schedule III.

# SCHEDULE V
## Includes codeine-containing analgesics

A The drug or other substance has a low potential for abuse relative to the drugs or other substances in Schedule IV.

B The drug or other substance has a currently accepted medical use in treatment in the United States.

C Abuse of the drug or other substance may lead to limited physical dependence or psychological dependence relative to the drugs or other substances in Schedule IV.

# The World's Most Comprehensive and Detailed Strain Guides

## CANNABIS SATIVA
The Essential Guide to the World's Finest Marijuana Strains
Edited by S.T. Oner
With an introduction by Greg Green

## CANNABIS INDICA
The Essential Guide to the World's Finest Marijuana Strains
Edited by S.T. Oner
With an introduction by Greg Green

Volume 1
Green Candy Press

## CANNABIS SATIVA
The Essential Guide to the World's Finest Marijuana Strains
Edited by S.T. Oner
With an introduction by Mel Thomas

Volume 2
Green Candy Press

## CANNABIS INDICA
The Essential Guide to the World's Finest Marijuana Strains
Edited by S.T. Oner
With an introduction by Mel Thomas

Volume 2
Green Candy Press

**Each Book Features 100 Amazing Strains from 100 Amazing Breeders!**

**No other strain guide series has featured this many breeders and strains before!**